# How To Analyze People:

## Analyzing and Reading People using Proven Methods of Human Psychology, Body Language, People Skills, Social Skills, Nonverbal Communication, Personality Patterns and Human Needs

### By Brian Masters

**Legal notice**

## More from Brian Masters

Other books by Brian Masters
http://www.amazon.com/author/brianmasters

Follow Brian on Twitter
@brianmasterskdp

# Free bonus

Thank you so much for taking the time to read this book. I know that by applying what you will learn in this book you can make truly amazing changes in your life by analyzing the people around you!

As my gift to you, please accept a free bonus ebook aimed at making you a more confident, persuasive, and effective public speaker. The thought of pubic speaking is known to cause even more fear and anxiety than the thought of death! If you've ever been in a situation where speaking in front of people made you nervous, check out this bonus ebook *available now at no additional cost to you* and learn some tips that will help you next time around!

**Claim your free ebook and get instant access by using the link at the back of this book!**

# Table of Contents

# Introduction

## The Benefits of Analyzing People (Why is it Important?)

Analyzing people is not only fun. It also provides several benefits. If you can read people, you can understand them better. You will also know more about a person without directly asking for information. It also lets you gain someone's trust, increase rapport, make better decisions about others and understand how people relate to each other.

Learning how to analyze people also allows you to evaluate the cohesiveness of a group. You will know who to trust, what to expect from others, and whether someone is telling you the truth or lying. Analyzing people is also beneficial if you want to protect yourself from dangerous and unreliable people. It also prevents you from being read by someone.

This book will give you effective steps to analyze people and gain the benefits mentioned above. It will teach you:

- The basic strategy for analyzing people

*Forms*

- Body language analysis

- Facial expression analysis

- Voice analysis

- Language analysis

- "Mind-reading"

- Cold-reading

- Background analysis

- Detecting deceit

- Protecting yourself from readers

You will need additional research and lots of practice to become adept in reading people, but once you are done with this book, you can start applying the skills immediately.

# Chapter 1 - Basic Strategy for Analyzing People

Analyzing people includes these basic categories:

Appearance

- Cleanliness

- Clothing

- Accessories

- Grooming

- Health status

*1ST LOOK IMPRESSION*

Body language

- Body positioning

- Posture

- Facial expressions

- Gestures

*DEEPER MEANING*

Voice quality

- Volume

- Tone

- Rhythm

Words

- What he/she talks about

- Words used    *H mmmm*

- How they are said

Actions

- What he/she usually does    *W HO ARE*
*YOU REALLY...*

- How he/she spends time

Background

*NEIGHBORHOOD*
*CLIQUE/HOBBY*    From the information you gathered from
the person (from observations and
conversations)

- From research and statistics

Gather as much info as you can from someone whom you are planning to analyze, so you can better understand him. Avoid focusing only on one or two traits. Doing so may cause bias in your interpretations.

# Chapter 2 - How to Analyze Body Language?

A person's mind and body are closely linked to each other, so by observing body language (positioning, posture and gestures), you can decipher his inner state.

Reading body language is a bit tricky since it can have several meanings. For example, crossing the arms can be interpreted as defensiveness, but it may also mean that the person is feeling cold. To avoid misinterpretations, do the following:

Look for body language clusters

*CLUSTERS (ONE OR 2 MOVEMENTS)*

Emotions and states of mind exhibit groups of signals. Even though someone may not demonstrate all of them, he may give off a couple of signs that say the same thing. The more of these clusters you detect, the stronger the message becomes.

*BE AWARE*

Detect signals that happen at the same time

Movements that happen simultaneously are often caused by the same stimulus. Observe synchronous motions to have a clearer understanding of what goes on in a person's mind.

Consider these factors before interpreting body language:

- Environmental factors

- Physical and psychological condition

- Illnesses

- Influence of drugs or medication

- Culture

- Situation

- Activity

_FACTORS_

Think about how these can influence someone's body language. Do not confuse these with what he is currently thinking or feeling.

With that being said, let's go to the particulars of body language analysis.

Proxemics

Proxemics is the study of the distances between individuals. There are certain zones

16

that are usually designated for particular interactions:

- Public zone (more than 12 feet) for public speaking, addressing a large group of people  *PUBLIC SPEAKING*

- Social-consultative zone (4 – 12 feet): formal interactions  *PROFESSIONAL*

- Casual-personal zone (18 inches – 4 feet): informal relations usually with friends and relatives  *FRIENDS*

- Intimate (0 – 18 inches): for lovers, very close friends and family members  *FAMILY & LOVE*

Remember that the measurements given above may vary depending on culture. It is also possible that a person who stayed long enough in a particular place will demonstrate proxemics in that area.

For example, Japan's casual zone measures 36 inches, North America is 18 inches, Western Europe is 15 inches, while the Middle East is 10 inches.

Before reading a person based on proxemics, consider the situation first. Are you in a crowded place? Is it hot or cold? Are the

*FACTORS*
*: CROWD / TEMP*
*ETC.*

people afraid? Is the speaker talking without a microphone? Does the culture encourage closeness or distance?

By considering external factors, you can tell people's relationships with each other based on the distances between them. You can also tell whether a person respects conventions and other's spaces. Being too close or too far than expected may signal problems.

*TELL RELATIONSHIP BY DISTANCE*

Body Angling

Face to face - When people face each other, it can mean confrontation or intimacy.

Side by side - This position makes it hard to see each other's entire faces. This is also done focus on one thing or come into terms with the same issue.

To quickly determine interest:

Watch where the upper torso and/or feet are pointing. They are usually directed to the person or object of interest. If they are facing you, they are interested in what you have to say. If their torso and/or feet are facing the door or away from you, they probably want to leave.

*IF TORSO, FEET POINTED AWAY = NO INTEREST*

## Openness/Closedness

Body language clusters can be categorized as open or closed. Switching from open to closed and vice versa is important since it indicates a change of attitude. Before making conclusions based on openness or closedness, look for other confirmation signals and check for other factors that cause the body language.

## Open Body Language

OPEN = INTIMATE

This signifies straightforwardness, confidence, acceptance, trust and relaxation.

The (arms and legs are not crossed.) The palms are relaxed and may be open. The person makes (eye contact) or looks around the environment. He may loosen his clothes.

Take note that open body language may also mean aggression. A hostile person may try to show his strength by not making defensive gestures. Watch out for clenched fists and sudden movements to confirm whether anger is present. Prolonged eye contact may be

MAY MEAN AGGRESSIVE ( CONTROL

considered as either a threat or attraction depending on other signals.

HUG
= PALMS
ROUNDED
SIDE BY
SIDE

When the arms are rounded and the palms are held side by side, he may want to give you a hug. If he cares for you, gestures will be gentle and slow.

If he lowers his body and holds the palm upwards, he is showing supplication. He is subconsciously showing you that he is unarmed so you don't have to fight.

Closed Body Language

DEFENSE / THREATENED / HIDING

This is usually interpreted as defensiveness but like open body language, it can mean other things as well. A person may be defensive when he dislikes something, is threatened, or desires to hide something.

TENSION

Arms and/or legs are crossed. Hands may be closed, folded or clasped. They may also cross on the wrists. The shoulders and arms may show tension. He may hold on to something for support. There is minimal eye contact. The head is turned away from you or tucked down.

HEAD TURNED OR TUCKED

Cold temperatures can cause closed body language. Consider how cold it is before interpreting this as defensiveness. *Could be caused by cold*

Some people display closed body language when they are relaxed. Notice their breathing pattern and facial expression to know if this is the case.

Emblems

Emblems are signals with specific meanings in a group or culture. People in a clique can recognize each other and communicate with the use of emblems. You can sometimes tell what group one belongs to through the emblems he uses.

Ex. Gang signs, secret signals

Illustrators

Illustrators are gestures that help describe what a person is talking about. These are less consciously controlled than emblems so they can reveal his true nature.

When he uses a lot of illustrators, he may be engaged with the topic, but it may also mean that he is not really careful about how he acts. On the other hand, if someone does not make use of them, it may mean that he lacks interest or is uncomfortable about the topic.

Illustrators can also give away what he is really thinking about. For example, if he says one thing but his actions describe a different thing, it may mean that he is lying or covering up something.

Ex. Sweeping gestures (broadness), making a chopping motion against one palm of the hand (decisiveness), putting the tips of the thumb and fingers together (precision)

Affect Displays

Affect displays are demonstrations of emotion. These tend to be more spontaneous rather than controlled.

Ex. Hugging one's self (sad), rubbing hands (excited), covering mouth (surprised)

Regulators

Regulators are gestures used to control the flow of the discussion. When these are not used, it may mean that people are not really listening or they don't want to participate in the discussion. Those who are not conscious of regulators may talk excessively. Distractedness

22

and impatience are clues that someone feels that it is his turn to speak.

Ex. Leaning forward, opening mouth, displaying illustrators, fidgeting, raising one hand    REGULATORS = INTEREST

Adaptors

Adaptors are unconscious actions done to cope with stress or anxiety. These are useful if you want to determine if someone is lying to you or if he feels uncomfortable about something.

Ex. Scratching, shaking the leg, fidgeting, grooming the hair, biting the lip, bouncing on the chair

# Chapter 3 - How to Analyze Facial Expressions

Facial expressions reveal emotions and thoughts. Regardless of age, race and culture, people generally look alike when they feel certain emotions:

Happy – A smile is the most obvious sign of happiness. Genuine happiness is revealed when the eye muscles also move, forming wrinkles at the corners. When the eyes remain still or narrow, the person may be pretending to be happy out of respect or sarcasm.

*SMILE & EYES*

Sad – The unique sign of sadness is when the inner parts of the eyebrows are drawn upwards and inwards. Mouth corners may be downturned. The bottom lip may protrude.

Angry – Anger causes the eyebrows to lower and meet. Eyes often squint. Lips may be compressed, with the jaw clenched or the lower jaw pushing forward. *SQUINT*

Afraid – Eyebrows are raised and may create wrinkles on the forehead. The eyes are wide *WIDE* open revealing a lot of white around the irises. The mouth may open.

Surprised – Similar to being afraid, but the person may take a sharp inhale.

Disgusted – The nose is wrinkled as if the person has smelled something bad. The upper lip curls upward so the teeth are exposed. Eyebrows are drawn together and lowered like in anger.

Eye movement

Eye movements can reveal what a person is thinking about, whether he is recalling something or making something up, whether he is lying, and what he is feeling. These can also control the flow of the conversation or direct people's attention to something.

Visual

- Recalling images (seeing a memory): upwards left

- Constructing images (creating an image in the mind): upwards right

Auditory

- Recalling sounds (voices, songs, etc.): sideways left

- Constructing sounds (composing a song or fabricating an conversation): sideways right

Kinesthetic

- Feeling something such as an emotion or sensation *EYES DOWN RIGHT = EMOTION*

- Eyes move downwards right

Internal Dialogue

- Having a conversation with one's self

- Eyes move downwards left

Direct gaze: self-confidence, trust *) TRUST*

Avoidant gaze: doubt, insecurity

Looking down: respect, submission, guilt, shame, fear *FLIRTING = PEELING THRU EYELASHES*

Looking up: remembering something (visual recall) or flirting (when done with head tilted down and peering through eyelashes).

Moving eyes side to side: can mean lying or being distracted by something.  Darting eyes *) DISTRACTED* may mean that the person is suspicious or distressed.

*Eyes Blink = Attraction* (handwritten margin note) Rapid blinking eyes: attraction (especially when combined with grooming gestures) or irritation (when done along with annoyance signals).

Narrowing eyes: can mean evaluating something or disapproval.

*Glances Reveal Want* (handwritten margin note) Glancing: where the person glances at may reveal what he wants at that time. Observe where the eyes move when he is not currently doing anything.

- If the person stares at the door, he may want to leave the room.

- If he focuses on somebody else, he may be attracted to that person.

- If he looks down, he may be tired or uninterested.

Staring intently at you may either mean interest or hostility depending on other body signals.

Pupil Size

- Large eye pupils - The person likes what he is seeing or he is being honest

- Small eye pupils - He dislikes what he is seeing or he may be telling a lie

- Fluctuating eye pupil size – He is unsure or anxious

When observing pupil size, make sure to consider the brightness or darkness of the room. Also, make sure that he is not under the influence of pupil-altering substances such as alcohol or recreational drugs.

# Chapter 4 - How to Analyze People Based on How they Talk

The way people talk tells a lot about what goes on in their head. These are some signs that point to what someone is accessing mentally.

Visual (seeing mental images)

- Talks fast

- Voice may be high-pitched

- Breathing is rapid and shallow

*MENTAL IMAGES*

Auditory (listening to voices or sounds in the mind)

- Voice has a pleasant melodic quality

*SOUND*

- Breathing is done from the middle of the chest

Internal Dialogue (talking to himself/herself)

- Jaw may slightly move in response to words spoken in the head

- May look like he is deep in thought, such as gripping or stroking the chin

Kinesthetic (having emotions/sensations in their mind)

SLOW-MO BEEP

- Talks slowly, often with prolonged gaps between words

- Voice may be low-pitched

- Breathing is full and from the lower belly

Voice Qualities

The voice reveals the person's emotional state. Even if he tries to appear normal, you can tell what he really feels by listening to how he talks.

Emotional

- The voice may quiver or crack when he is emotional.

- A voice that rises in tone may mean doubt or questioning.

- When the inflection rises and falls, the speaker may be sarcastic.

- A disgusted person talks fast in a low pitched voice.

- Anger is vocalized in a low pitch and a loud volume.

- When both volume and pitch rises, he is really angry.

- Talking rapidly with a varying pitch denotes excitement.

- A high pitch voice and frequent pauses express sadness.

- Speaking slowly in a monotone is a sign of defeat.

Words Used

*I = Self Conclous*

Pay attention to the spoken words. These can sometimes tell you more about a person.

Excessive use of the pronoun "I" reveal self-consciousness and inner troubles. Those who are more secure with themselves often use the pronoun less. Because of this, those who are lower in status often use a lot of I's when communicating with their superiors, while high ranking people use few to no I's when talking with subordinates. High status people also use more "we" and "you" words.

A liar may avoid using "I", and use general statements, instead. For example, instead of saying, "I did not steal the group's funds", he will say "Anyone who truly cares for the group will never do such a thing!" In comparison, honest people will be more generous in using exclusive words such as "without" and "but" and negations such as "no", "never", and "none."

Women use personal pronouns such as "I", "me", and "mine" more frequently than men. They also use more third-person pronouns like "he", "she", and "they." In general, woman are better at relating with others, thus they naturally talk more about relationships, people and social concerns. Men are prone to using more articles such as "it", "the", "a" and "an" and they tend to favor discussions focused on concrete objects and impersonal issues.

Personal pronouns will give you an idea of how a person sees himself in relation to others. As mentioned, those saying "I" more frequently do so out of a greater degree of self-focus. You can also determine whether someone focuses more on males or females by the frequency of his "he's" and "she's." When referring to a group, watch out if "we/us" or "they" is used.

34

This will tell you whether he feels like a member of that group or not.

A person who is unsure will use words and phrases such as "I think", "It seems", and "maybe." More decisive individuals will go straight to the point – an indecisive person will say, "I think I want to go ahead," while a confident person will say "I'll go ahead." People who are certain about things like mentioning certainty words like "always", "never", and "absolutely."

*(Handwritten annotations: "UNSURE", "DECISIVE")*

Analyze what the person writes about. Are there a lot of emotional words? What feeling is predominant? How are sentiments expressed? Does the person focus more on positivity or negativity?

Observe words describing thought processes. Does the person make generalizations or is he after precision? Is he fond of mentioning the cause and effect of things? Does he try to be understood by saying words such as "I mean" or "you know"? Are the words used common or are they technical, abstract, or flowery?

Which among the drives of affiliation (relationships), achievement, power, reward and risk are most talked about? Is there a greater focus on certain life areas such as health, food, work, money, home, family, friends, leisure, spirituality, etc.? Do his words center on the present, past or future? You can decipher one's motivations and interests by looking at these details.

Does he use formal or informal language? When using informal language, are there fillers, slang words, or netspeak included? Does he frequently use assent words (ex. "right?" or "isn't it?") that ask for agreement? This will give you an idea of his temperament and preoccupations.

*IMPORTANT*

What does the person talk about? People usually talk about things they find important. Pay attention to what he brings up in a conversation. Look at his social media posts. His topics will tell you about his priorities and interests, giving you an idea about his personality.

You will know whether someone likes you if his language changes and become more similar to yours. This tendency is observable among people who are in love with each other and talk/chat regularly to one another. If you notice someone copying your language

*COPY LANGUAGE = ATTRACTION*

patterns, it could be that he admires you in some way.

These are only some of the things you can get from the way a person communicates. Interacting more with people and giving your full attention to them will let you gather additional details.

FULL ATTENTION

●

# Chapter 5 - Gaining a Deeper Understanding of Yourself to Analyze Others Accurately

Understanding yourself helps you analyze others more accurately because humans are similar to each other. Knowing yourself well also helps you know what your biases are, thus, you can be more objective in making your analysis.

Inaccurate beliefs and prejudices color our perception of other people. If you want to make correct judgements, train yourself to be a critical thinker. Increase your knowledge about different kinds of people to eliminate prejudices. Know what your expectations are so you can separate them from what you should perceive.

Be familiar with cognitive biases so you can avoid them. For example: the halo effect is a social bias where a positive trait of a person makes him appear to be completely pleasant even if he also has negative traits. The projection bias is the tendency to assume that others share your values and beliefs. The actor-observer bias makes one assume that other people do things because of their personality while he acts according to his situation. There are many biases such as the ones mentioned. Learn as many as you can and catch yourself whenever you are becoming biased.

*OBSERVE YOURSELF*

Observe yourself closely. Study your internal processes and their effects on your behaviour. What makes you do things? How do certain life situations affect your actions? Watch yourself in the mirror or record yourself. How do you look and sound like when you are happy, angry, lying, etc.?

Be aware of how you affect other people. How do you present yourself? How do you treat the other person? Do you express some kind of emotion? Do not mistake people's responses to your actions as an overall reflection of their character.

Think of how you interact with different people – a partner, love interest, child, parent, relative, friend, classmate, co-worker, teammate, colleague, rival, enemy, boss, subordinate, neighbour, acquaintance, role model, celebrity, foreigner, stranger, annoying person, scary person, etc. Remember what went on in your mind, what you felt, and how you behaved. Take a look at pictures or videos if they're available.

Reflect on your beliefs, values, needs and motivations. How do they affect the things you do? Are they obvious in the things you talk and write about? When you analyze yourself regularly, you will get used to analyzing others as well.

# Chapter 6 - Cold Reading
## People at First Glance

Cold reading is a set of techniques that enable you to gather information from someone without him knowing about it. In comparison, hot reading is gathering details through direct questioning.

Some cold readers pretend to have psychic powers to distract people from what they are actually doing. Next time you see a magician, psychic, or mentalist say things that he isn't supposed to know, you can suspect that he used cold reading techniques.

Cold reading involves the following: *COLD READING*

- Reading body language *BODY*
- Making guesses based on appearance *APPEARANCES*
- Asking questions or giving general statements that subtly elicit information *SUBTLE QUESTIONS*
- Using information gathered from observations, questioning and statistics

*CONNECT THE DOTS*

*ADJUST*

- Adjusting statements depending on the target's responses

- Delivering 'escape statements' that save the reader from misses

*SUMMARIZE*

- Summarizing the reading by mentioning only the correct guesses and omitting the wrong ones

If you want to cold read by sight, you have to know how to decipher body language. You also need to pay attention to the details of his appearance. More importantly, you must have a wide knowledge on what to expect from those who have certain characteristics. Studying psychology, sociology, cultures and demographics will help you immensely with this.

*CHARACTERISTICS*

For example, just by estimating a person's age, you will gain some insights about his possible capabilities, interests, preoccupations and struggles. School-age children are likely to experience a lot of peer pressure. Retirees are often concerned about their health and mortality. Young adults may be struggling to balance their work and family life. Every characteristic of a person has effects on his life, so you can derive a lot of information about him from his traits.

You may classify a person broadly into categories such as businessman, intellectual, wife and mother, retiree, student, conformist, etc. It helps to have an idea of how it's like to be part of a particular group. For this, you may need to do some research, observations and interviews. The more you know about them, the better you can read people.

Regarding demographics, there are numerous statistics on age groups, genders, income brackets, religions, educational levels, nationalities, ethnicities, and more. You can gain plenty of insights about different kinds of people from these figures.

.NO STEREOTYPES

Avoid stereotyping – this may bias your reading. The basic ideas that are associated with stereotypes are sometimes true, but don't rely on them completely. Always be observant and non-judgmental. Be willing to revise your beliefs about someone when you gather evidence that conflicts with those beliefs.

Be like Sherlock Holmes when observing appearances – pay attention to every single detail and create a story out of each one. A

EVERY
DETAIL IS
A STORY

wedding ring is obviously a sign that a person is married. If he is not wearing a ring yet there's a light band where a ring used to be, it may mean that the person just had a divorce or that he is having an affair.

When evaluating someone, consider all possibilities first then eliminate those that aren't likely. Build your conclusions out of the available evidence. Never fall into the trap of making a hasty conclusion and finding details that 'confirm' it. This is known as a "confirmation bias".

FEEDBACK

Cold reading in a conversation allows you to modify your guesses according to the responses of your target. You don't have to ask him directly whether you have guessed correctly. You can tell whether you are right when the target looks excited (for a believer) or anxious (for a sceptic), and you may be wrong if he is disappointed or smug. Getting feedback will help improve your cold reading skills, so seek it out whenever you can.

# Chapter 7 - Advanced Strategies for Analyzing People

Advanced strategies for analyzing people involve learning beyond what you can physically observe.

Know his background:

- What his childhood was like    BACKGROUND

- Where he grew up

- The culture of the place he spent most of his time in

- Whether he has an active social life or is more of a loner

These things will tell you his normal behavior. This will also give you an idea about his values and beliefs.

Determine what he is in need of. These are some needs that are common to most people:

- Survival

- Security

- Comfort

- Love

- Belongingness

- Relationships

- Interactions with others

- Self-esteem

- Recognition

- Reward

- Power

- Good feelings

- Knowledge

- Learning

- Understanding

- Stimulation

- Growth

- Self-expression

- Aesthetic pursuits

- Achievement

- Self-actualization

- Significance

- Meaning in life

- Spirituality

- Service

- Contribution

- Self-transcendence

ACTIVELEY
STIRVVING?

COMPENSATE?

Is he actively striving for something? What is the purpose of his actions? Is he trying to compensate for something that is lacking?

How does he prioritize things? Is he neglecting some needs? If so, how does this affect language and behavior?

What is his general nature? Does he do good or bad to other people? People who are negative may have issues in their own lives.  GENERAL NATURE Some of their needs may not be met so they focus more on themselves, instead of thinking about others' needs. Their discomfort may cause them to be hostile. On the other hand, those who have no unmet needs and have resolved their issues can afford to be positive and kind. Helpful people may also have experienced being in the position of those they are helping.

What kind of crowd do they hang out with? If a person regularly interacts with a group, it means that he is comfortable there for a particular reason. People tend to like others who are similar to them.

OPEN
MINDED

If he goes with several different kinds of groups, you may consider him as having a flexible character. He may be open-minded, caring and experienced in dealing with people.

If he is a loner, it could be that he does not feel the need to socialize. He may also be uncomfortable when in social situations. Being alone may also point out to an above average intelligence. Smart people tend to be happier when they have fewer friends because they prefer to work on something important rather than participate in social gatherings.

What kind of clothes is he wearing? What music does he listen to? Do people around the same age as he is have the same fashion and music styles? Every genre of music and fashion tells something about the nature of the person who likes them. If the person has tastes that are different from those of his age group, it may mean that he is intellectually older or younger than his years. Otherwise, it may also signify that he is a non-conformist.

Since a person is a complex being, there is no end to what you can read if you are patient enough to explore. However, you must consider his need for privacy. Not everyone appreciates being read. Some will even feel that you are violating their privacy when you do so. When you read, it will be better if you seek his consent first. Otherwise, don't let him know that you're reading him like a book.

Now that you know how reading a person is done, you can protect yourself by learning how **KEEP** to control your actions. Keep yourself calm by **CALM** breathing evenly and not ruminating on thoughts that put you on edge – this will prevent emotions from leaking out.

Avoid moving as much as possible, for you give away your thoughts through your gestures and changes of position, but of course, do not look too stiff or the reader will know that you are being defensive. Move from time to time to make yourself comfortable, but mind your movements so they don't give away valuable information.

**BE SMOOTH**

To protect your identity, do not reveal too much of yourself especially online where anyone can look for your posts. If you want to express your innermost thoughts, write in a diary instead and keep this hidden. This is most important if there are people who want to know more about you to use the information against you.

# Chapter 8 - Can you Fake Body Language?

People may try to fake body language to avoid revealing the truth of what they really think and feel.

Deception

Being deceitful is harder than being honest because it requires more effort to make up a story than remember what really happened. Aside from looking at the eyes (remember, looking right means making something up) and observing language patterns, you can also detect dishonesty if there is tension, anxiety and distractedness.

*Looking right = deceit* (handwritten annotation)

Tension – sweating, muscle twitches (such as around the eyes and mouth), abrupt movements and changes in the tone and speed of the voice

Anxiety signals – biting the lip or nails, patting his/her own head, hiding the hands in pockets, fidgety movements, looking away, focusing on unusual areas

Distracted – lying and manipulation requires more effort in thinking, thus, a deceiver may talk more slowly or pause a lot. He may lose track of what goes on around him as he focuses on his thoughts, thus, he may over-react or under-react.

Watch for incongruence

Having incongruent signals means having body language, voice qualities, and/or words that are not in harmony with each other. For example, a person may pretend to be honest by opening his palm and uncrossing arms and legs, but you will notice that he is avoiding the pronoun "I" and that his shoulders are tense. In general, incongruence signifies that he is trying to hide something and/or that he is experiencing an inner conflict.

For micro expressions

Micro expressions are rapid expressions of emotions on the face. These are important because they often show one's true feelings. These usually happen when he is trying to control his body language.

MICRO EXPRESSIONS

## Faking your own body language

You may try faking your body language to throw people off. Practice body language signals so you can act when you need to. Pay extra attention to the deception signs mentioned above so that you don't commit them. Strive to be as natural as possible by having thoughts and emotions that support the message you want to send. You don't have to keep them indefinitely, only while you're being observed.

# Conclusion

Remember that this book is only a guide for you to start analyzing people. Relying on book knowledge provides a foundation to build upon with real-life practice and applications of the techniques you've learned in this book.

Make use of every opportunity to analyze people and take notes if you can. Record your hits and misses. Learn from your mistakes and research about the things you still need to know. Talk to those who are good people analyzers – you will learn a lot from them.

Reading people is a skill that you can grow every day if you keep at it. Although it takes commitment, the benefits will be worth the effort. Good luck on your journey to improve your understanding of other people and yourself.

# Free bonus

Thank you so much for taking the time to read this book. I know that by applying what you've learned in this book you can make truly amazing changes in your life!

As my gift to you, please accept a free bonus ebook aimed at making you a more confident, persuasive, and effective public speaker. The thought of pubic speaking is known to cause even more fear and anxiety than the thought of death! If you've ever been in a situation where speaking in front of people made you nervous, check out this bonus ebook *available now at no additional cost to you* and learn some tips that will help you next time around!

**Claim your free ebook and get instant access here:**

## www.boostlifenow.com

Made in the USA
Lexington, KY
27 October 2016